Anonymus

Catalogue and Description of a very large Collection of prehistoric

Relics obtained in the Cliff Houses and Caves of southeastern Utah

Anonymus

Catalogue and Description of a very large Collection of prehistoric Relics obtained in the Cliff Houses and Caves of southeastern Utah

ISBN/EAN: 9783742802248

Manufactured in Europe, USA, Canada, Australia, Japa

Cover: Foto ©Thomas Meinert / pixelio.de

Manufactured and distributed by brebook publishing software (www.brebook.com)

Anonymus

Catalogue and Description of a very large Collection of prehistoric Relics obtained in the Cliff Houses and Caves of southeastern Utah

CATALOGUE AND DESCRIPTION

OF A

VERY LARGE COLLECTION

OF

PREHISTORIC RELICS,

OBTAINED IN THE CLIFF HOUSES AND CAVES

OF SOUTHEASTERN UTAH.

THIS COLLECTION

IS FOR SALE.

ADDRESS

Mc LOYD & GRAHAM.

P. O. BOX 312, DURANGO, COLO.

EXPLORERS

OF

PREHISTORIC RUINS

AND COLLECTORS

OF

RELICS.

1894.

CLIFF DWELLERS RELICS.

The Cliff Dwellers ruins are located in south wes-
tern Colorado and the adjacent parts of Utah, New
Mexico, and Arizona, with some scattered through
Old Mexico.

The Cliff Dwellings are built in wind worn caves,
and are so well protected by the over-hanging cliffs,
that no moisture ever reaches them. This accounts,
to a large extent, for the fine state of preservation
of this collection As a rule those articles not found
with human remains, were covered, with debris, to
the depth of from six inches to as much as eight feet.

All articles not otherwise described were found in
the refuse or sweepings from the houses. As the
map of that part of Utah from which this collection
was obtained is almost a blank, we will say that
Grand Gulch has its source in the Elk mountains
its course being south-west, it terminates in the
canon of the Rio San Juan, some fifty miles above
the junction of that river with the Colorado. It is
about sixty miles long, with an average depth of
near fifteen hundred feet. we found many ruins in
this canon.

Lake canon is a tributary of the Rio Colorado.
The junction with that stream, being some twenty
miles above the mouth of the Rio San Juan. The
canon is about twenty five miles long, and very
deep. It is on the East side of the Colorado. Many
relics were obtained here.

Red Canon is tributary to the Colorado on the East, and enters that river some fiftteen miles above the mouth of Lake Canon. Only a few ruins were found in it.

White Canon is also atributary of the Colorado river on the East, and joins it near Dandy crossing, San Juan County Utah. This canon is some seventy miles long, and the exploring party only found one place where animals could be taken in to it. There are prehistoric ruins in it.

A few ruins have been found in the Canon of the Colorado River, but they are not so large or numerous as in the side canons.

GROUP A

CONSISTING OF HUMAN REMAINS.

Usuly the larger humad remains were buried in a doubled up posture, the knees drawn up against the chest, the clothing being left on the body.

Not enough bodies are found around their houses, and uhder the over-hanging cliffs, to indicate that their custom was to bury in these places. No land marks leading to the discovery of the general burial places of the Cliff Dwellers have yet been found.

Some of the skulls in this collection were obtained from underground rooms, that have been excavated in the clay bottoms of the caves. The largest of these rooms are as much as twenty two feet in diameter; they have b en filled in with a hes and other refuse, and the stone Cliff houses constructed over them. The heads taken from these rooms are of natural form, never having been changed by pressure.

No skulls of this shape are found in the stone Cliff houses that are in the same caves, and no flattened skulls are found in the underground rooms.

In some of the caves portions of bodies were found in the debris, as if they had been carried there by animals. In cases of this kind no other articles were found with them.

Articles found in the rooms beneath the Cliff houses, are, to some extent, different from those obtained in the stone houses above, In the notes at the head of each group, mention is made of those articles peculiar to the underground rooms.

No 1. Headless mummy, of female child, that was found in Lake Canon; with it found Nos. 20 C, and 26 I. We are unable to determine if head was taken off before or after burial.

No 2. A well preserved mummy, five feet six inches in length; with it found Nos. 13, 14, 15 and 26, C, 22, 23, and 24, D, 16, 17, 48 and 50, E, 5, 6, 27, 28 and 45, I, 10, K, and 16 and 10, H. This mummy was found burried in one of the underground rooms in a cave in Grand Gulch. The articles found with it were around the body in various positions, no attention, apparently, having been given to what position they were placed in, only they were near or against the body .There is a cliff house in this cave.

No. 3. A well preserved mummy of a child, about 3 feet high; found in a cave in Grand Gulch. It is wrapped in fur cloth, and deer skins that have been tanned with the hair on; with it were found Nos. 9 and 10 C, 12 E, and 15 J. The hair on the head of this child is of a red cast.

No. 4. Mummy of a very small child, that was found in a basket ,- 23 C,- with another basket ,- 12 C,- turned over it; was found in a cave in Colorado River Canon, just above the mouth of the San Juan.

No. 5. A mummy of child, wrapped in fur cloth and buckskin, and tied on a pappoose frame; with it found Nos. 1, C, 3, 4, 5, E, 9 and 44 I, 3, 6, 7, and 8 J. This was found in a cave in Red Canon.

No. 6, well preserved headless mummy of a male, that, in life, must have been six feet in height; was found in a cave in White Canon. With it were found Nos. 2, 3, 5 and 25 C, 14, 15 and 17 D, 6, 7, 10, 13, 14, 15 and 41 E, 4 F, 15, 16, 19, 20 and 46 I.

In this instance, as in others, where mummies are found without heads, it is very difficult to determine if heads were taken off before or after burial; as animals have dug holes in the ground and may have destroyed or taken away parts of the bodies.

No. 7. A well preserved mummy of a man that has been about six feet in height; was found in a underground room in a cave in Grand Gulch. With it were found Nos. 7, 8, 11 and 27 C, 9, 18 and 19 D, 8, 9, 12, 19. 20, 21 aud 36 E, 13, 14 and 15 H, 1, 3, 7, 13 and 47 I, and 27 J. There is a cliff house in this cave.

No. 8. Mummified lower arm and hand; found in the debris in a cave in White Canon.

No. 9. Mummified leg and foot, from a cave in Red Canon; was found in debris.

No. 10. Mummified arm and hand; was found in the debris in a cave in Lake Canon.

No. 11. Mummified foot and leg; found in a cave in White Canon.

No. 12. Mummified hand, and arm; found in a cave in Grand Gulch.

No. 13. Same as No. 12, and was found in same cave.

No. 14. A small mummified leg and foot; with a sandal on the foot. Was found in a cave in Lake Canon.

No. 15. Skeleton hand and arm; was found in a cave in Grand Gulch.

No. 16. Mummified leg and foot.

The above Nos. from 8 to 16, inclusive, were found in the debris in the various caves, and, no doubt, had been moved by animals.

No. 17. Mummified head; found in a cave in Lake Canon; with it found Nos. 4 C, 22 E, and 12 H. No other portions of the body were found, and nothing to indicate that any other part had been buried with it.

No. 18. A childs skull, from cave in Grand Gulch.

No. 19. Childs head, partly mummified; was found in a cave in Lake Canon. with it were found Nos. 24 C, and 43 I.

No. 20. small skull, found in Lake Canon; with it 19 C, 49 E, and 12 I.

No. 2I. Skull, from a cave in White Canon.

No. 22. Skull, from cave in Red Canon; with it found No. 22 C.

Nc. 23· Skull, from cave in White Canon; with it found No. 52 of this group.

No. 24- Skull,from cave in Grand Gulch; with it found No. 14 J.

No. 25. Skull of Cliff Dweller; was found in a cave in Grand Gulch. With it were found Nos. 12, 29 and 30 B, 39 and 48 E, 6 H, and 6 K.

No. 26. Mummitied head, from a cave in Red Canon; with it found No. 57 I.

No. 27. Skull, from Red Canon; with it found No. 17 J.

No. 28. Mummified head, from an under-ground room in a cave in White Canon; No. 30 of this group was with it. A feather robe – 49 I – was spread over them.

No. 29. Skull, found in a cave in Lake Canon.

No. 30. Mummified head, with gray hair on it; was found in a cave in Lake Canon.

No. 31. Skull, found in same cave as No. 30 of this group.

No. 32. Skull of a cliff Dweller; was found in a cave in White Canon. with it, Nos. 13 and 28 B, 4 and 9 H, 22 and 29 I, and 7 K.

No. 33. Head, partly Mummified; was found in same under-ground room as Nos. 16 to 27 B.

No. 34. Skull, from cave in White Canon.

No. 35. Mummified head, found in a cave in White Canon.

No. 36. Skull, from cave in White Canon.

No. 37 Skull, found in same under-ground room as Nos. 16 to 27 B, and 30 of this group.

No. 38. Skull of small child; was found in a cave in White Canon. With it were found Nos. 37 I, 21 and 23 J.

No. 39. Mummified head of a small child; hair is yet on it. was found in a cave in Lake Canon. With it Nos. 2 and 3 H, 11 I, and 22 J.

No. 40. Mummified head, from a cave in Red Canon; with it were found Nos. 20 and 25 D, 52 E, 11 H, and 8 I.

No. 41. Large skull, from cave in Red Canon.

No. 42. Skull, from same cave as No. 41 of this group.

No. 43. Mummified head, from a cave in Grand Gulch; with it found Nos. 14 and 48 I, and 16 J. The hair on this head is partly gray.

No. 44. Skull, from White Canon.

No. 45. Skull, from cave in Colorado River Canon.

No. 46. Mummified head, from a cave in Lake canon; has gray hair on it. With it No. 10 J.

No. 47. Skull, from a cave in Grand Gulch; with it 18 and 20 J.

No. 48. Consists of 16 lower jaws, collected from the various caves where work was done. They were generaly found in the debris, and may have been carried there by animals.

No. 49. Two bunches of gray hair, were found in a cave in White Canon.

No. 50. Consists of 11 bunches of red hair; from the various caves mentioned.

No. 51. Twenty bunches of hair; from the various caves in which work was done.

No. 52. A large bunch of hair, tied with a string, just as found; with it No. 23. of this group.

No. 53. Part of scalp, with the hair on it; was found in a cave in Lake Canon.

No. 54. Mummified hand and arm, from cave in Grand Gulch.

GROUP B.

POTTERY, ETC.

There are some three classes of pottery represented in this collection. The commonly accepted theory
as to the way in which the coiled ware was made, is
that by taking a rope or fillet of clay and wrapping it
round and round, and crimping it on with the finger
or some pointed instrument,- thus leaving indentations on the outer surface,- they were able to construct
a vessel of the size and form desired. The inner surface was smoothed, and the vessel hardened by fire.

Very large cooking vessels were made in this way,
and also smaller vases. Almost every vase of this
ware has been blackened by fire. Evidently they
would stand considerable heat.

The second kind,- of which there are only a very
few pieces in this collection,- is the ordinary glazed
and painted ware, so commonly found in the valley
and other ruins of this section. So much has been
found and placed on exhibition, that we do not con-
sider it so valuable as other kinds. The designs
painted on this class of ware are generally geometrical, and the vessel is often artistic in shape. Few
life forms,in this class of ware, have been found in
cliff houses,but are not uncommon in the valley
ruins.

The third kind of pottery is very valuable, less

than 50 pieces having been found up to date, and those in the under-ground rooms that have been mentioned as being underneath the cliff dwellings, and in the same caves. It is a very crude unglazed ware, some of the bowls showing the imprint of the baskets, in which they were formed. Nos. 16 to 27 inclusive are of this kind of ware. Most of the large coil vases were found where they had buried them in the floors; evidently for storage of seeds, etc. Measurements for circumference were made around largest part of vessels.

No. 1. Coil vase, 18 inches in height and 50 inches at largest circumference; has bands of uncrimped coils about every two inches. Was found in a cave in Grand Gulch.

No. 2. Coil vase, 13 inches in height and 40 inches in circumference. After this vase was made, but before it was burnt, lines about one inch apart, were made by drawing a sharp pointed instrument over the outer surface, from top to bottom. Also found in a cave in Grand Gulch.

No. 3. Coil vase, 16 inches in height and 49 inches in circumference; was found in a cave in White Canon.

No. 4. Coil vase, 16 inches in height and 49 inches in circumference. It is marked like No. 2 of this group. Was found in Grand Gulch.

No. 5. Coil vase, 13 inches in height and 47 inches in circumference; was fonnd in a cave in Grand

Gulch.

No. 6. Coil vase, 14 inches in height and 42 inches in circumference. Has a net-work of yucca blades or leaves around the outside, they are fastened to a bark ring placed under the vase, and to a piece of large twine that is tied around the vessel under the rim. This was found in a cave in Grand Gulch.

No. 7. Coil vase, 13 inches in height and 42 inches in circumference. A very fine vessel, and nicely shows the coil and indentations. Was found in a cave in Lake Canon.

No 8. Coil vase, 15 inches in height and 45 inches in circumference. Was found in Lake Canon.

No. 9. Coil vase, 10 inches in height and 31 inches in circumference. In it was found the small basket-No.6. group C. From a cave in the Canon of the Colorado.

No. 10. Coil vase, 10 inches in height and 33 inches in circumference. Was found in the Colorado River Canon.

No. 11. Coil vase, 12 inches in height and 34 inches in circumference. Was found in Red Canon.

No. 12. Coil vase, 8 inches in height and 28 inches in circumference. This was buried with No. 25 group A. and contained the seeds, No. 6 group K.

No. 13. Coil vase, 7 inches in height and 20 inches in circumference. It is enclosed in a net-work of yucca leaves or blades. Was found with No, 32 group A. and contained the seeds, No. 7 group K.

No. 14. Coil vase, 7 inches in height and 20 inches in circumference. It has two projections just under the rim, they are adout 5-8 of an inch in length, and 1-2 inch apart. Evidently has had same kind of projections on opposite side, but they are broken off. This was found in a cave in White Canon.

No. 15. A pottery disk, 2 1-2 inches in diameter; has small hole in the center. Was found in the debris in a cave in Grand Gulch.

Nos. 16 to 27 inclusive, were found in a large under-ground room in a cave in Grand Gulch, and were from 6 to 8 feet below the surface. The room had been filled in with refuse, and a stone Cliff house constructed over it. Skulls Nos. 33 and 37 were found in the same room, but apparently the pottery had not been buried with them, as it was in another part of the room.

No. 16, An odd shaped dipper, with round handle about ten inches in length.

No. 17. A shallow dipper, with flat handle.

No. 18. An oval shaped dish, about 5 inches in diameter.

No. 19- A round dish, about two inches deep, and six inches in diameter. Shows the imprint of basket on the outside.

No. 20. Peculiar shaped vessel. that is about 3 inches wide, 6 1-2 inches in length, and comes to a point at the ends; the opening in the top is about 1-2 inch in width, and 3 1-2 inches in length. May have been used for a lamp.

No. 21. Dish, 3 inches deep and 8 inches in diam eter. It has a large knob on each side, and a lip on one edge. Shows the imprint of a basket on outer surface.

No. 22. A flat ladle, 8 1.2 inches in length. Has been painted.

No. 23. Dish about 2 1-2 inches deep, and 6 inches in diameter.

No. 24. Shallow dish or plate, 7 inches in diameter. Has been painted.

No. 25. Small painted bowl or cup, with two projections on the rim.

No. 26. Dish about 4 inches in diameter; has six sharp-pointed projections around the rim.

No. 27. Flat ladle or paddle, 4 inches in width and 11 inches in length. Has a flat handle, and has been painted.

No. 28. A small painted mug or pitcher, that was found with the skull No. 32 group A.

No. 29. Small painted dish, that was found with skull No. 25 group A.

No. 30. A dipper, with part of handle broken off. Was found with skull No. 25 group A.

No. 31. Very small unbaked bowl, that was found

in a cave in Colorado River Canon.

No. 32. A piece of pottery that resembles the spout of a sprinkling can. Was found in a cave in Grand Gulch.

. . . .

GROUP C.

WICKER—WORK. ETC.

These pre-historic races made some very fine baskets, often weaving them so closely that they were almost water-tight. By using material of different colors – generally willows– they worked in geometrical designs, thus producing a very pleasing effect.

The material used in making some of these baskets has not been determined.

The large flat baskets or platters, – this name is used for the reason that they resemble plates – have only been found in the under-ground rooms that have been mentioned.

No. 1 plain shallow basket, about 15 inches in diameter at the top. Was found with mummy No. 5 group A.

No. 2. A loosely woven basket, made of yucca blades; it is about 6 inches deep and 15 inches in diameter at the top. This was found with the mummy No. 6 group A.

No. 3. A very well preserved flat basket or platter, about 1 1-2 inches in depth and 19 inches in diameter at the top; is very closely woven, and has dark line around the rim. This was found with No. 6 group A.

No. 4. Plain basket, about 14 inches in diameter at the top. Was found with the skull No. 17 group A.

No. 5. A closely woven basket, with flat bottom about 5 inches in diameter. The sides are about 3 inches in height, and are drawn in so as to form an opening in the top about 2 1-2 inches in diameter. This was found with mummy No 6 group A.

No. 6. A loosely woven basket, that will hold about one pint. Was found in the coil vase No. 9 group B.

No. 7. Basket, closely woven in different colors, thus forming geometrical designs; it is 7 inches in diameter, and 3 inches in depth. Was found with the mummy No. 7 group A

No. 8 Closely woven basket, that is 4 inches in depth and 15 inches in diameter. Was found with mummy No. 7 group A.

No. 9. Closely woven and well preserved basket, with flat bottom, flaring sides and fancy geometrical designs. 1t is 5 inches in depth and 17 1-2 inches in diameter. Found with No. 3 group A.

No. 10. Closely woven basket bottom, 9 inches in diameter. Found with No. 3 group A.

No. 11. Basket, with dark border; it is 2 1-2 inches

in depth, and 8 inches in diameter. Found with No. 7 group A.

No. 12. Basket, 3 inches deep and 12 inches in diameter. Was turned over mummy No. 4 group A.

No. 13. A very fine and well preserved basket, with fancy designs worked in it. Found with No. 2 group A.

No. 14. Pouch, made of yucca blades loosely woven; is 3 inches in diameter and 7 in length. Found with No. 2 group A.

No. 15. The bottom of one of the large baskets, such as were used in carrying heavy burdens; has geometrical figures woven in. Was found with No. 2 Group B.

No. 16. Closely woven basket, 2 inches deep and 10 inches in diameter at the top. Was found in a cave in White Canon.

No. 17. Saucer-shaped basket, 8 inches across the top. Was found in a cave in Grand Gulch.

No 18. Very small saucer-shaped basket, 3 1-2 inches in diameter at top; it is closely woven in different colors, and is well preserved. Was found in a cave in Red canon.

No. 19. A flat basket or platter, that is not very well preserved, the rim having been broken off and fastened on again. Was found with skull No. 20 Group A.

No. 20. Large basket, closely woven, with designs in dark colors; it is 19 1-2 inches across the top this is very well preserved, and is a fine specimen. Was found with No. 1 Group A.

No. 21. Basket, 4 1-2 inches deep and 11 inches in diameter at top. It is in good condition, and as the bottom has been mended, it shows nicely how they did that kind of work. Was found in a cave in Grand Gulch.

No. 22. Saucer shaped basket, that is very poorly woven; is about 16 inches in diameter at the top. Was found with skull No. 22 Group A.

No. 23. Saucer-shaped basket, 17 inches in diameter at top. In this was found the mummy No. 4 Group A. The basket No. 12 was turned over it.

No 24 A saucer-shaped basket, 14 inches in diameter at the top; it is closely woven in designs that do not show very well. Was found with skull No. 19 Group A.

No. 25. Saucer-shaped basket, 20 inches in diameter. A part of the designs that are woven in are black, but others have evidently faded. This was found with mummy No. 6 Group A.

No. 26 Well preserved flat basket, or platter, 20 inches in diameter at top; has dark band around the edge. A very fine specimen, and was found with No. 2 Group A.

No. 27. An unfinished basket, 15 1-2 inches in diameter. Found with the mummy No. 7 Group A.

No. 28. Saucer-shaped basket, 7 inches in diameter. This was filled with gray hair, and was found in the Colorado River Canon.

No. 29. A very large basket, evidently made for carrying heavy burdens on the back; it is closely woven in colored designs, and is about 3 feet in diameter. Was found on top of skulls Nos. 28 and 30 Group A.

No. 30. An oval shaped frame, with the back and part of the front covered with a net-work of yucca blades. Was found in a cave in Grand Gulch.

. . . .

GROUP D.

STONE AND STONE IMPLEMENTS.

It is the opinion of those who have explored the ruins of this section of the country, that all stone implements found belong to the neolithic or advanced stone age; there may be, however a few exceptions to this rule. No metal of any kind has been found, but we have found copper and iron ores. Evidently they did not understand smelting them.

No. 1. Stone, such as was used to grind grain in; it is 10 inches wide 17 inches long and 3 inches thick, and is hollowed ont in center. Was found in Grand Gulch.

No. 2. Stone, such as used in the hand when grinding grain; it is 4x5 inches. Was fonnd in Grand Gulch.

No. 3. Grooved hammer, that is 8 1-2 x 4 1 2 x 1 1-2 inches. Found in a cave in White Canon.

No. 4. Grooved hammer, 7 1-2 inches in length, 2 1-2 inches in width. From a cave in Colorado River Canon.

No. 5. Round stone, 4 1-2 inches in diameter; has a small cavity in it, as if intended for a mortar. Found in Grand Gulch.

No. 6. Unfinished stone ax. Was found in a cave Lake Canon.

No. 7. Stone ax, with part of the handle on it. From a cave in Colorado River Canon.

No. 8. A small round stone; use unknown.

No. 9. A thin stone, about 3 inches square; has a Maltese cross cut in it. Found buried with the mummy No. 7 Group A.

No. 10. A thin stone, about 3x4 inches, with a peculiar shaped cross cut in it. Was found in a cave in Colorado River Canon, above the mouth of the Rio San Juan. It was in the debris, and was covered about two feet. There is small cliff house in the cave.

No. 11. Celt or skinning knife, 8 inches in length. Was found in a cave in Red Canon.

No. 12. A thin smooth stone, shaped like the sandals No 2 in Group F. It is 11 inches in length, 4 inches in width at one end, and 6 at the other. Use unknown. Was found in a cave in Lake Canon.

No. 13. Grooved sledge, 3 1-2 x 6 x 7 inches. Was found in cave in Grand Gulch.

No. 14. A flint arrow point, with a wooden shaft attached. Was buried with No. 6 Group A.

No. 15. Flint point, much like 14, and was also buried with No. 6 Group A.

No. 16. Flint drill point, fastened in the end of a round stick, 1-2 inch in diameter, and 6 inches in length. Must have been revolved with a bow or between the hands. Was found in the debris in a cave in Lake Canon.

No. 17. Spear head, that has the point broken off. Was found with No. 6 Group A.

Nos. 18 & 19. Large arrow points. Found with the mummy No. 7 Group A.

No. 20. Point of spear head, Found with skull No. 40 Group A.

No. 21. Consists of two arrow points, and one drill point. Found with No. 45 Group A.

No. 22. A flint scraper. Found with No. 2 Group A.

No. 23. Flint spear point. With No. 2 A.

No. 24. Flint arrow point. With No. 2 A.

No. 25. An arrow point. Found with No. 40 Group A.

No. 26 Consists of 34 arrow points, and parts of points, that were found in the various caves in which work was done.

· · · · · · · · · · · · · · · · · · ·

GROUP E.

Such sticks as are represented by Nos. 52. 53, 54 and 55, have only been found in under-ground rooms, or buried with skeletons with heads of the same shape as those found in such rooms. We presume that the small boards like Nos. 42 to 49 inclusive, are peculiar to this race, as we never find them buried with the flattened skulls, or in the cliff houses. When not otherwise mentioned, articles are from the debris in the caves, and such caves usually have cliff houses in them.

No. 1. Part of pappoose board, 6 inches wide, 8 inches long. Found with No. 3 A.

No. 2. A piece of wood, 4 inches wide and 12 inches long; use unknown. Was found with No. 3 A.

No. 3. Part of pappoose board, 3 inches wide, 14 inches long. Was found with No. 5 A.

No. 4. Circular piece of wood, about 4 1-2 inches in diameter; use unknown. Was found with No. 5 A

No. 5. Piece of board, 7 inches long, 4 to 6 inches wide; use unknown. With No. 5 A.

No. 6. A cup-shaped vessel, made from the knot of a tree. It is about 6 inches in diameter. Was found with No. 6 A.

No. 7. A board, 1-2 inch thick, 7 inches wide and 16 1-2 inches long; evidently the back piece of a cradle or pappoose board. Found with No. 6 A.

No. 8. Board, same size as No. 7, but not finished.
Found with No. 7 A.

No. 9. Board, about 9 inches wide and 16 inches
long; may have been used as a platter. Found with
No. 7. A.

No. 10. Round smooth oak club, 25 inches in
length, 1 3-4 inches in diameter at large end; has a
knob on small end, to prevent it slipping through
the hand; may have been used as a war club. Found
with No. 6 A.

No. 11. Wooden wedge, with yucca blades tied
around the top, to prevent it splitting when ham-
mered on. Found in a cave in White Canon. .

No. 12. Farm implement, 27 inches in length.
Found with No. 7 A.

No. 13. Farm implement. With No. 6 A.

No. 14. Seed planter, 36 inches long. Found
with No. 6 A.

No. 15. Broken stick, 1-2 inch in diameter and 19
inches long; one end is hollowed out and wrapped
with sinew. Use unknown. Was found with No. 6 A.

No. 16. Round pointed farm implement, 21 inches
in length. Found with No. 2 A.

No. 17. Wooden fleshing knife, 16 inches long
1 1-4 inches wide. Found with No. 2 A.

No. 18. Walking stick, 34 inches in length; has
been made by procuring a stick with a natural crook
to fit the hand. Was found with No. 2 A.

No. 19. Walking stick, 37 1-2 inches in length; .

has curved top, and is wrapped with sinew in two places. Was found with No. 7 A.

No. 20. Farm implement, 28 inches in length; is very smooth. Found with No. 7 A.

No. 21. A round smooth stick, 25 1-2 inches in length; is wrapped with sinew in several places. Found with No 7 A.

No. 22. Flat farm implement, 1 1-2 inches in width, and 33 inches in length. Found with No. 17 Group A.

No. 23. Small piece of board.

No. 24. Small board.

No. 25. Double pointed awl.

No. 26. Small wooden scraper.

No. 27. Fire stick.

No. 28 Wooden wedge; much the same as No.11.

No. 29. Wooden awl, about 15 inches long.

No. 30. Fire stick, such as was used with the bow, or revolved between the hands.

No. 31. Side board of a cradle, or pappoose board.

No. 32 Fire stick; such as the stick No. 4 of this group, was revolved in. Has a number of holes burnt into it.

No 33. Wooden arrow point, with notch for inserting a flint point.

No. 34 Small stick; about 11 inches long; point rounded and knots smoothed down. Use unknown.

No. 35, Wooden arrow point. shouldered to fit a reed.

No. 36. A musical imstrument, that resembles an ordinary fife, except that it has only four holes. This was found with No. 7 A.

No. 37. A round wooden awl.

No. 38. Small piece of wood showing where it has been cut with a flint knife, or other implement'

No. 39. Wooden arrow point, made to fit in the end of a reed. Found with No. 25 A.

No. 40. Small board.

No. 41. A peculiar shaped implement, 3 inches wide, 24 inches long; end bent up so as to form a kind of paddle. one side is painted red, white and black. The use is unknown. It was found with the mummy No. 6 A.

No. 42. Small piece of very smooth board.

No. 43. Small board.

No 44. Small piece of board.

Nos. 45, 46, 47. Small boards.

No. 48 Board, found with No. 25 A.

No. 49. Board, found with No. 20 A.

No. 50. Throwing stick, about 23 inches in length. The shaft is of some hard wood. At one end is a shallow gutter and a hook to receive the end of a spear shaft. At the grip end, about 4 inches from extremity is a loop on either side of the stick. These loops were made by splitting pieces of rawhide, and sliding them down the proper distance on the stick' forming loops less than an inch in diameter by bringing the projecting ends of the rawhide and seizing them fast to the shaft.

This was found with the mummy No. 2. A, and was so placed that the end with the loops on was near the right hand, the other end being near the head.

No. 51. Small bow, about 20 inches long, such as were used to revolve drills and fire sticks. Was found in a cave in White Canon.

No. 52. Consists of 75 small sticks, about 12 to 14 inches in length. Each stick is wrapped with thread or sinews about 3 inches from the small end. Use unknown. Was found with No. 40 A.

No. 53. Consists of 35 small sticks, about six inches in length, with one or two grooves cut around them at each end. Use unknown.

No. 54 Consists of 40 small sticks, similar to No. 52.

No. 55. A small stick, similar to No. 53.

. . . .

GROUP F.

SANDALS, ETC.

Sandals are often found in the refuse or sweepings from the houses, and generally show some wear. We are of the opinion that those with square toes were made by the race who inhabited the underground rooms. This view is formed from often finding them buried with mummies of that race, and is strengthened by the fact that we have found none in caves where such ruins do not exist. Where not otherwise mentioned, they are from debris and sweepings in the caves.

No. 1. Consists of 52 sandals, made of unsplit yucca blades, Most of them are in an excellent state of preservation.

No. 2. Consists of 22 sandals, made of split yucca blades.

No, 3. Five sandals, made of split yucca blades, the main or largest strands are woven across them.

No. 4. Five sandals tied together as found. They are woven in different colors, aud have square toes, and buckskin fringe. Were found with No. 6 A.

No. 5. Consists of 33 sandals, most of which have ornamental fringe, and are made with square tots.

No. 6. Small unfinished sandal.

No. 7. Very finely woven sandal, that is as good as when first made, and looks as if it had never been worn; has square toe, ornamental fringe, and the strings used for fastening it on the foot are complete.

No. 8. Very finely woven sandal, with square toe, buckskin fringe, and red border; is complete except heel strings. This is wrapped in buckskin, and evidently has never been worn. A splendid specimen.

No. 9. Woven sandal, with square toe, and ornamental fringe made of strings of different colors; is complete, with strings etc. Has never been worn, and is as good as when made.

No. 10. Consists of two large sandals, with cedar bark and corn husks in them, thus showing how they were used in cold weather.

No. 11. Buckskin sandal, with douple heel and toe.

No. 12. Small buckskin moccasin.

No. 13. Buckskin sandal, of double thickness.

No. 14. Small buckskin sandal, that is of double thickness.

No. 15. Plaited sandal, that is in an excellent state of preservation, and has complete set of strings for fastening it on the foot.

Nos. 16 to 22. Much the same as No. 15, except they are without full set of strings.

No. 23. Sandal, made by taking two old sandals, one of which had been worn through at the heel, and the other at the toe, and sewing them together.

No. 24. Pair of large sandals, with strings etc. complete.

No. 25. Sandal, that has been patched; is very long and narrow.

No. 26. Loosely woven sandal, that is as good as new.

No. 27. Sandal, made for a very small child; the toe is ornamented with red thread.

No. 28. Baby's sandal that is loosely woven, but is complete.

No. 29. Extremely wide sandal.

No. 30. Sandal, with corn husks in it to protect

the foot.

Nos. 31 to 33. Baby's sandals.

No. 34. sandal, made of twine that had been used as the foundation of feather cloth.

No. 35. Sandal, made of turkey feathers.

Nos. 36 to 40. Pieces of sandals.

Nos. 41 to 43. Sandals they have commenced, but never completed.

No. 44. Sandal, in which part of the material used is hair.

No. 45. A mat, that is made of cedar bark, is about two feet square.

No. 46. A mat, made of yucca blades, is two by three feet.

No. 47. A large buckskin moccasin.

. . . .

GROUP G.

BONE IMPLEMENTS, ETC.

These implements are usually found in the debris near the houses, and all articles in this group were so found, unless otherwise mentioned. We can see no difference between those found in caves in which there are underground rooms, and where there are only cliff houses.

No. 1. Bone skinning knife.

No. 2. Bone fife, with six finger holes. Was found with No. 27 A.

No. 3. Horn of female mountain sheep. It has a hole through the small end, and may have been used for a drinking cup.

No. 4. Bone knife, much the shape of a razor.

No. 5. Large bone awl.

No. 6. Small bone drawing knife.

No. 7. A bone on which they have done some work, evidently with the intention of making a drawiug knife.

No. 8. Large bone awl.

No 9. Combination knife and awl.

No. 10. Awl, made of the rib of an animal.

No. 11. Consists of 12 bone awls, of various sizes.

No. 12. A small piece of ivory.

No. 13. Flat piece of bone, that shows use.

No. 14. Two bone needles, one of which is 1 inch in length, and the other 3 1-2.

... .

GROUP H.

ORNAMENTS, ETC.

Judging by the position in which we find the beads when buried with the dead, they must have been worn around the neck, wrists, and at the ears.

A few have been found in the mouths of the mummies of the race with the natural shaped heads, but we think they came there by accident, and do not indicate that it was a custom to place them there.

No. 1. String of beads, made of shells of a reddish color; is 14 inches in length. Was founnd with No. 2 A.

No. 2. String of beads, made of seeds or berries. Was found with No. 39 A.

No. 3. String of small pottery beads.

No. 4. String of beads, made of white shells that are about 1-2 inch long. Found with No. 32 A.

No. 5. String of shell beads.

No. 6. Very long string of bone beads. Was found with No. 25 A.

No. 7. String of small pottery beads.

No. 8. A bunch of twine with three beads on it.

No. 9. A string of six beads of different kinds. Was found with No. 32 A.

No. 10. Small string of beads, with a piece of turquoise near the middle. Must have been worn at the ear. Found with No. 2 A.

No. 11. Two bone beads, about 1 inch long. Was found with No. 40 A.

No. 12. String of beads, of various kinds and shapes. Was found with No. 17 A.

No. 13· Thirty inch string of shell beads. These shells are from 1-2 io 2 inches in length. Was found with No. 7 A.

No. 14. Five inch string of beads, Was found with No. 7 A.

No. 15. A stone disk, with a hole in the center; is of a yellowish color, and is 1 inch in diameter. Was found on the breast of No. 7 A.

No. 16. Stone bead or charm.

No. 17. Piece of shell bead or charm.

No. 18. A peculiar shaped stone. Use unknown.

. . . .

GROUP I.

TEXTILE FABRICS, ETC.

The feather cloth, much of which is mentioned in this group, was made by stripping the feathers off the quills with a thin fibre adhering; wrapping this fiber around cotton or yucca cord with the feather part out, thus forming rolls of feathers. These rolls being woven together formed the feather cloth. They also made a cloth in much the same way by using the fur and hair of animals.

Where not otherwise mentioned, articles in this group were found in the debris in the caves.

Such seamless sacks as mentioned in this group, so far as we know, have never been found buried with the race with flattened skulls. They are generally bell shaped, the bottom being round and much larger than the top. Some of them are woven with stripes of different colors around them, thus producing a pleasing effect.

No. 1. Seamless sack, that has been cut down the side, so that it could be spread over the mummy No. 7 A. It is 20 inches in length.

No. 2. Sack that has been partly burned.

No. 3. Part of a seamless sack, Was found with No. 7 A.

No. 4. Seamless ack. Was found with No. 1 A.

No. 5. Unfinished seamless sack. Was found with No. 2 A.

No. 6. Large and well preserved seamless sack, that has been ripped from top to bottom. Was found spread over No. 2 A.

No. 7. Large piece of buckskin, tanned with the hair on. Was found spread over the mummy No. 7 A.

No. 8. Piece of buckskin. Found with No. 40 A.

No. 9. Fawn skin, tanned with the hair on it. Found with No. 5 A.

No. 10. Piece of buckskin. With No. 46 A.

No. 11. ..   .. No. 39 A.

No 12. ..   .. No. 20 A.

No. 13. ..   .. No. 7 A.

No. 14 ..   .. No. 43 A.

No. 15. Large piece of buckskin. With No. 6 A.

No. 16. Large piece of buckskin, tanned with the hair on.

No. 17. Small piece of cotton cloth.

No. 18. Consists of three small sacks, or pouches.

No. 19. Small sack, that contains some corn meal. Was found with No. 6 A.

No. 20. Seamless sack, 12 inches in length; contains some corn meal. Found with No. 6 A.

No. 21. Two small buckskin pouches.

No. 22. Buckskin pouch, with some corn meal in it. Found with No. 32 A.

No. 23. Small buckskin pouch, made by sewing three pieces together.

No. 24. Part of a seamless sack.

No. 25. Small buckskin pouch, that contains a substance resembling yellow ochre.

No. 26. Piece of buckskin. Found with No. 1 A.

No. 27. Large buckskin. Found with No. 2 A.

No. 28. ..   ..

No. 29. Squirrel skin pouch. With No. 32 A.

No. 30. Piece of buckskin, that has had some yellow substance tied up in it.

Nos. 31 and 32. Pieces of cotton cloth.

No. 33. Cased skins of two small animals. They have been tanned with the hair on, and then used as sacks or pouches.

No. 34. Bunch of new or unused twine, such as forms the foundation of the feather cloth.

No. 35. Strings, evidently used as a body belt.

No. 36. Part of a cotton band.

No. 37. Part of a badger skin, that has been tanned with the hair on. Found with No. 38 A.

No. 38. Hair band, that is 2 feet long and 2 inches wide.

No. 39. Skein of hair thread.

No. 40. Belt made of hair twine.

No. 41. Part of a woven band, with designs painted on it.

No. 42. Part of a hair band.

No. 43. Garment, made of fur cloth. It looks like a baby's bib. Found with No. 19 A.

No. 44. Same kind of a garment as No. 43, but is made of feather cloth. Found with No. 5 A.

No. 45. A feather cloth robe, that is in good condition. Size 32 x 36 inches. Found with No. 2 A.

No. 46. Feather cloth robe, 28 x 36 inches. Was found with No. 6 A.

No. 47· Feather cloth robe, 27 x 36 inches. Has most of the feathers worn off. Found with No 7 A.

No. 48. A piece of feather cloth. Was found with No. 43 A.

No. 49. Feather robe, that is 45 x 45 inches.

No. 50. Apron made of fine strings.

No. 51. Piece of fur or feather cloth, that has the wrapping that was on the twine worn off. It is 24 x 24 inches.

No. 52. Small piece of cotton cloth, that shows fancy stitching.

• • • • • • • • • • • • • • • • • • • •

GROUP J.

We have never found stone pipes, such as mentioned in this group, buried with any of the race with flattened skulls. They are made in the shape of a cigar holder, and are of various kinds of stone.

The rings or mats mentioned, are of different kinds of material, and are such as were used to support convex bottomed vessels on the floor, or while carrying them on the head.

If not otherwise mentioned, articles were found in the refuse from the houses.

No. 1. Small bundle of canes. With No. 3 A.

No. 2. Small roll of cedar bark, bound with yucca blades. This was evidently used to carry fire from place to place.

No. 3. Piece of corn cob, with a quill inserted in the end.

No. 4. Roll of cedar bark, much like No. 2, and used for the same purpose.

No. 5. Bunches of feathers, that are tied to buckskin strings; then all the strings bound together with sinew. Use unknown. Was found with No. 3 A.

No. 6. Prepared yucca, such as was used in making twine and rope.

No. 7. Two short sticks, crossed and tied with grass. Found with No. 5 A.

No. 8. Baby's rattle, made of mountain sheep hoofs.

No. 9. Bundle of stiff grass stems, used for a comb.

No. 10. An unfinished basket.

No. 11. Two bundles of turkey feathers.

No 12. Bundle of black feathers.

No. 13. Bundle of short strings.

No. 14. Stone pipe, three inches in length. Found with No. 24 A.

No. 15. Bundle of yucca blades.

No. 16. Stone pipe, two inches in length. Was found with No. 43 A.

No. 17. Stone pipe, that seems to have never been used. Found with No. 27 A.

No. 18. Stone pipe, that has been fractured and mended by binding it with sinews. Was found with No. 47 A.

No. 19. Pottery pipe, two inches in length.

No. 20· Pottery pipe, 3 1·2 inches in length.

No. 21. Pappoose cradle, of wicker work. Was found with No. 38 A.

No. 22. Same as No. 21, except that the rim is covered with buckskin. Found with No. 39 A.

No. 23. An article made by weaving small canes together, with hair and yucca strings. It is 4 inches wide and 2 feet long. Was found with No. 38 A.

No 24. Bunch of yucca.

Nos. 25 and 26. Two rope snares, such as were

used to snare small animals. Found with No. 7 A.

No. 27. Large bunch of prepared yucca, for making rope.

No. 28. Hair string.

No. 29. Woven band, about two feet long.

No. 30. Bunch of yucca.

No 31. Three gourds, about the size of oranges.

No. 32. Skein of twine.

No. 33. Two strings wrapped with fur; are about 12 inches in length, and are tied together at one end. The other ends have small bunches of hair tied on them.

No. 34. Ring, 2 1-2 inches in diameter. It is made of strings.

No. 35. Ring or mat, such as was used to support vessels. It is made of cedar bark.

No. 36. Ring or mat, made of yucca fibre.

No, 37. Resembles a bowstring, and is made of sinews.

No. 38. Bunch of prepared yucca fibre.

No. 39. Platted rope, 4 feet in length.

No. 40. Piece of very dark colored rope.

No. 41. Piece of rope, showing square plat.

No. 42. Rope, made of gray hair.

No. 43. Cane pipe stem.

No. 44. Hair rope, 15 inches long.

No. 45. Small rope, with hair strings fastened in the ends.

No. 46. Rope, 6 feet in length.

No. 47. Large bunch of strings, of various kinds.

No. 48. Large bunch of fur and feather cloth strings.

No. 49. Hair rope, 4 1-2 feet in length.

No. 50. Black paint.

No. 51. Several pieces of copper ore.

No. 52. Powdered black paint.

No. 53. Green paint.

No. 54. Large vessel, made from the rind of a squash.

No. 55. A broken piece of pottery, that has been used to heat pitch in.

No. 56. White, brown and yellow paint.

No. 57. Several small stones of different colors.

. . . .

GROUP K.

SEEDS ETC.

We had intended to catalogue the seeds in the miscellaneous group, but as they have a special interest for some collectors, concluded to make of them a separate group.

Although many attemps have been made, - some of which were under very favorable conditions- no one has succeeded in germinating any of these seeds.

Where they were not found in vessels, they came

from small holes dug in the clay bottoms of the caves. Where these holes had been covered with flat stones, the seeds were sometimes protected from small animals.

No. 1. About 1-2 gal. of yellow corn. Was found in No. 7 B.

No. 2. About 2 gals. of yellow corn, that is not so large as No. 1. Found in No. 4 B.

No. 3. About 1 gal. of large red corn. Was found in No. 8 B.

No. 4. Twenty ears, and pieces of ears, of corn.

No. 5. Five ears of red corn.

No. 6. About 1-2 gal. of small black seeds. Have not determined the kind. Found in the coil vase No. 12 B.

No. 7. About 1 1-2 pint of small brown seeds. Kind not determined. Found in the coil vase No. 13 B.

No. 8. One quart of pumpkin or squash seeds. Found in No. 9 B.

No. 9. One pint of small seeds. Found in No. 14 B

No. 10. Pinon nuts. Were found with No. 2 A.

No. 11. One pint of pumpkin or squash seeds.

No. 12. Beans, and other seeds.

. . . .

www.ingramcontent.com/pod-product-compliance
Lightning Source LLC
Chambersburg PA
CBHW021549270326
41930CB00008B/1427